Sweetheart

First published in 1998 by
Slow Dancer Press
59 Parliament Hill London NW3 2TB
England

©Tamar Yoseloff 1998

British Library Cataloguing-in-Publication Data. A catalogue record
for this book is available from The British Library.

ISBN 1 871033 47 0

Slow Dancer poetry titles are available in the U.K. through Signature Book
Representation distributed by Littlehampton Book Services and in the U.S.A.
& Canada through Dufour Editions inc, PO Box 7, Chester Springs,
PA 19425-0007.

Cover design: Keenan

Slow Dancer Logo: East Orange

Printed by Bell & Bain Ltd, Glasgow

This book is set in Elegant Garamond 10.5

Sweetheart

Tamar Yoseloff

Slow Dancer Press

Acknowledgements

Some poems in this collection first appeared in **Fun House**,
published by Slow Dancer Press in 1994.

Acknowledgments are also due to the following publications, in
which some of these poems appeared: *The Frogmore Papers, London
Magazine, Poetry London Newsletter, PN Review, The Richmond
Review* and *Seam*.

'Biology' was the winning poem in the 1995 London Writers'
Competition.

Grateful thanks to Sarah Boiling of Slow Dancer Press, and to John
Harvey, without whom this book would not have been possible.

For Andrew

Contents

Well then, stay here; but know,
When thou hast stayd and done thy most;
A naked thinking heart, that makes no show,
Is to a woman, but a kinde of Ghost;
How shall shee know my heart; or having none,
Know thee for one?
Practise may make her know some other part,
But take my word, shee doth not know a Heart.

John Donne

Selfridges

My mother held a wire basket in one hand,
my hand in the other. Occasionally she'd pause
to cross an item from her list as she plucked it
from the shelf. For a brief moment she released
her grip and I must have wandered off,
realised I was lost near the butcher's counter.
The full odour of fresh meat, blood and sawdust
hit me suddenly; I looked up to see hares, headless,
strung from metal hooks. I don't think I'd even seen
a hare alive. The butcher was hacking a flank into steaks,
the first cut opening the bright pink of the leg,
the second negotiating bone. But what stopped me
in my tracks was the offal, displayed lovingly on a bed
of lettuce and ice—lambs' kidneys, calves' livers,
sweetbreads, hearts—all the vitals without function.
Just then I felt my mother yank me by the wrist;
she must have scolded me for drifting away
in a strange store, a foreign country, I can't recall.
Twenty-five years later I can still see
those visceral hunks, served up like a delicacy,
indelicate, hearty, more real laid out there
than anything that beat inside me.

Asparagus

It was worth it just for the picking,
the clean sharp snap from the root.
No breeze, no sound, except the hum of cicadas
growing to a crescendo at the edge of the field.
By July I knew the first short stalks would soon appear;
it thrived in the August heat.

Someone before me had taken the trouble
to plant those neat rows. I hated to see it go to waste;
although I never liked the bitter aftertaste,
I'd gather armfuls. At dinner, I would eat the tips,
play with the stalks. I wasn't allowed to leave
until I'd eaten every bit.

But even in those days when I was rich
with asparagus, its season was brief. It would branch
into wild trees, the same time a chill was settling
on the edge of the air. I would shiver,
run inside to unearth a sweater, buried under a mound
of autumn clothes, sweet with mothballs.

Now it seems out of reach.
I could buy it at any supermarket, neatly trimmed,
tied in dainty bundles—it's not the same.
I long for the crisp, fresh explosion of green on my tongue,
the days I almost believed I had the power
to conjure it up from the ground.

In the Chelsea Physic Garden

To tell the truth, it's the names and not
the plants that get you, you thrill to Latin,
the *icus* and *atum*, the beauty of endings.
I like the juicy berries of the belladonna,
the shoo-fly with its little maracas, all
the strange and unloved weeds. Growing up,
the lullabies my mother sang were about
lost love and how sad the past could be,
later. No Rock a Bye, Baby, just the facts.

Now, I love her for it, for the names
she gave me, collections of constellations,
varieties of sea shells, the flowers
we'd pick out walking, bring home to dry.
I used to save abandoned baby birds,
frogs from snakes' jaws. It would always end
in tears. Forgive me, there are things I want
to say, but I have no words, just proper names,
more Latin, prosaic American slang.

In the fairy tale version, we are planted,
not side by side, as you might expect,
but in separate hemispheres, never to meet.
You the cool fern, adaptable to rainy climates,
and rain or shine, reliable. I'm the problem,
spiky, dangerous, the occasional flower,
poison of course. But exotic. Experts travel
miles to meet me. I dream of leaves, your
soft caress. I guess I'd slash you to bits.

The Butcher Cover

Stu Rosenberg was five foot two without
his Cuban heels. He'd met 'John' and 'Paul'
at the local synagogue. Their 'Ringo'
was an Irish kid, dyed his red hair jet black,
wore gold rings he'd bought cheap on Canal Street.

They played the convention circuit in Jersey,
most of the girls old enough to remember Wings,
did double bills with Nilsson and Mike McGear.
I heard them at the Meadowlands Hilton in '82;
if you closed your eyes, Stu could fool you.

He invited me to his room, ordered champagne
for *Harrison in 22*. We talked about the day
Lennon was shot, too young to remember JFK.
Then he showed me his prize, bought for a dollar
at a garage sale in Rahway: a real Butcher Cover.

I remember staring at their picture, younger then
than I am now, in their stained doctors' coats,
surrounded by bleeding chunks of meat,
George's hand spearing the head of a plastic doll
like a trophy. It was supposed to be a joke.

The record bosses issued an apology,
rushed them to Publicity. Suppliers were told to pulp;
some got lazy, pasted the new photo to the old sleeve.
Stu could see the image underneath, carefully steamed
the 'clean' one off, to uncover the real thing.

I was only sixteen, Stu a year older. He wanted
to take me to Liverpool, wanted me to meet his mother.
I never did either. My copy of *Yesterday and Today*
is torn where I tried to peel off the cover,
just board beneath. I don't listen to it anymore.

The Emergency Broadcast System

Sixth grade history—
and Mrs. Shramko unfurled her huge canvas map,
pulling it over the blackboard
like a shade on a window. The old world,
countries divided by colour: yellow Yugoslavia,
East Germany in brown and West in green,
the red mass of Russia staining the north,
the United States candy pink.

I thought the Cold War would be fought,
by definition, on the tundra, the ice floes
of Scandinavia, some arctic plain.
They could go away to sort things out,
no people, no civilisations to be destroyed.
I could see their tanks leaving tracks
in the perfect snow like B-movie monsters,
angry for something to attack.

America could stop worrying.
Those concrete bunkers still sometimes seen
in suburban backyards could be dismantled.
The voice of doom that came on the radio,
suddenly, in the middle of *Casey Casem* or *Dr. Demento*
could retire, never again to announce *this is ONLY a test*,
followed by that piercing signal,
preparing us to meet the end.

Driven

I remember the instructor saying
my three-point turn was perfect,
my parallel parking the best he'd ever seen.
He passed me and I never drove again.
Behind the wheel I was always five years old
in my scaled-down Speed Racer number 8,
circling the patio. Out on Route 18
I froze, imagined wrecks at roadsides,
scrap yards crammed with twisted metal,
a welder's flame reducing a chassis
to its elemental state. I want to preserve
the vistas that have opened to me in that *other* seat:

co-pilot; my friend in the driver's seat
of her dad's orange VW van. My first epic road trip
without my parents, who'd clocked up miles
of featureless highway, windows on central locking,
speedometer steady at 55. My friend and I
took off across Georgia, our goal to break
the cross-state record interrupted
for buckets of Popeye's chicken, black-eyed beans.
I can still see her, the wheel in one hand,
a crispy fried leg in the other,
picking it clean, flinging the bones out the window
at 75 miles per hour, licking her fingers one by one.
We parked at bars and truck stops, roadside shacks
that sold hot dogs and beer, full of men
named Billy Bob and Ray, who kept
cigarettes rolled up their sleeves and drove
Cadillacs and Chevys, big Detroit cars.
Like them, we believed we could drive endlessly,
the journey the thing itself, like Kerouac.
That was before the accident. Now her little MG
is tarpaulined in her garage like some rare beetle.

Since then, I have developed my role as navigator,
on interstate highways, on mountain roads
tugging a cliff's edge. At last I have found
the passenger's perfect country, throwing out
little villages like gifts along the way,
from Saffron Walden to Swaffham to Blakeney,
the road planting a bench where I would
most like to stretch my legs, admire the view.
I have come to love maps, the atlas open on my lap,
the country spread out before me, planning a route
to and from, the cross on the ordnance survey
translated into a tiny church, the lines of firs
into a whole forest. It's not as vast as America;
over time, with patience, you and I could see it all.
The little car can carry all our needs,
and as you drive I can fall asleep to Glenn Gould
working through the Goldberg Variations,
as night darkens the motorway, cat's eyes gleaming,
the headlights of passing cars guiding travellers
closer to their destinations.

The Cholera Graveyard

I.

In the railway office, your ex-lover
studies maps of North Yorkshire,
plots a course to and from London
along imaginary tracks.

From her window she can see
the station and the Great Northern,
where just last summer she made beds
all day, tucked hospital corners

perfectly, got paid in kind
words from travelling salesmen,
who drove up and down the M1
for a living. And you would roll

into town in a wreck named Bess,
the police noting your number plates,
just in case. You told her
your ancestors were famous thieves:

Dick Turpin, before him,
good Viking stock. She'd take you
to the Cholera Graveyard,
last trace of the Plague of 1832,

the contagions buried separately,
on the edge of town, you grew up
around them. You'd make love
so as not to wake the dead.

II.

You told me the story of your father,
a hero with a twirly moustache,
who was ploughed down by a fire engine,
speeding to the scene of a blaze.

You were only ten, so an uncle tried
to take his place, on Saturdays
he'd meet you at the bar walls,
and you'd walk full circle

past the Minster, the Shambles,
where your granny lived as a girl,
the station, the Cholera Graveyard,
scene of the Plague of 1832.

Still, you grew up with his presence
around you, no ghost or spook,
a sensation you could never explain.
You claim it was not chance,

the accident that left you unconscious;
seventeen, your first car, the same bend
in the same road that took him
exactly seven years to the day.

III.

In the time we were together
I never saw so many hearses.
Everyday there'd be one, some days
two. You told me we were doomed.

You started counting our omens,
wearing them around you like talismans:
all the freak rainstorms after love,
and then the unseasonable heat.

I said it could all be explained
by a hole in the ozone the size
of a country. But you didn't trust
scientists and their theories.

In the end we didn't last the winter,
but you gave me a love
of the unexplained. When we parted
I started running into accidents,

in a week I saw two fires, a car crash,
an avalanche. One day, a building fell
at my feet, an offering.
Now, I take it in my stride.

I remember a night so clear in my mind:
you talked about your childhood
as we sat in my darkened room,
one candle, the rain outside.

I will carry that with me
like you carry your father through
a city he wouldn't recognise now,
a ghost town, a lost cause.

Fleet

It flows beneath my feet, its subterranean banks
unseen. I glide blissfully through my day,
all liquid, like a fish. I can't understand
what gives this extra lift to my step, as if I'm floating,
and the cars drifting through Clerkenwell Green
are barges carrying sailors home from sea.

But an undercurrent sinks me at Islington:
I sense the bones of the old prison, the plague-dead
dumped straight from their beds, butchers' scraps
staining the water blood red. The old dark brick
shifts, the city groans in its foundations
and spits me out like a sour grape into the street.

Coin

You were not convinced
of authenticity: unearthed, they claimed,
in an ancient city, discovered beneath
a building site. I was entranced
by the face of a long-dead king,
his inscription rubbed smooth,

a mystery. I kept it in my pocket
for luck. Soon the little details
that had drawn us together
began to irritate. We fought over
the minutiae of who does what
and why. I blamed it on the coin.

I remembered the explorers
who'd found Tutankhamen's tomb
ignited his curse. I hurried my coin
to the riverbank, dropped it in.
It made a tiny splash, disappeared
into the deep black waters.

When we finally called it quits,
we split it all down the middle, yours
and mine, but couldn't divide
the only photograph of us together.
Let's toss for it, you said.
Neither one of us wanted a reminder.

My only regret is that coin:
in a hundred years, someone will scoop it
from the dry riverbed, a rare find,
hustle it to a museum. In the meantime,
it gleams amid rocks and rubble,
the very stuff on which kingdoms die.

Heart-butt

It is heavy in my hand,
the scent of metal and sweat
so similar to blood. Its bullet
could rip through cartilage and tissue,
shatter bone, no repairing
what it broke. But how elegant
the delicate scrollwork chiselled
into silver, dagmaker's name
carved on the lockplate, place and date:
the provenance of a gentleman.

I imagine he cut a fine figure,
ready to do battle for his land
or for the hand of a woman,
his pistol at full-cock.
But it was never fired: they know
by the wear on the flintlock.
Two hundred years later, his treasure
turned up in a Dundee pawnshop.

Unlike the lemon-butt
or lobe-butt, ramshorn or fishtail,
its pommel is shaped from the very thing
it aims for, drawn like a valentine
over the target, big and red,
ready to receive the hit.

Deer

You bring a flask of coffee, brittle cake
that breaks apart in our fingers.
You come here often, just to watch them
work the frozen earth
for what grass is left, heads bowed.

Here in the dark trees
almost anything is possible:
St. Eustace came upon a stag at bay
bearing the image of Christ on the cross
right between his antlers.

In shadow, you look like someone else.
I imagine the trajectory of our affair,
the dazzling week of all-night sex,
fizzling to a telephone call.
Our breath clouds before us, a hesitation.

I could go home before it starts,
to a cup of tea and *Now Voyager*.
I must learn patience, must wait for love
to transfigure me,
the forest ablaze with its light.

The Visible Man

displays his arteries and veins to me
like a road map. I trace the tangled route
to the heart, encased in plastic, every
piece of him defined, each contour scaled
down to size, a man in miniature.

There among memento mori, black jet
dripping like tears, a buffalo's head, a jungle
of taxidermy, he was still in his original box:
The wonders of the human body revealed!
complete with instructions for assembly,
an introduction to anatomy. I would
take him home, build him from scratch.

It was painstaking work, painting each artery,
hooking him up like a Christmas tree;
as he began to take shape, I could almost
sense the things he lacked: the smooth
skin covering hard muscle, a face made up
of all the faces I have loved, the eyes clear,
untroubled. I wanted to understand

everything: the flow of blood and semen,
the beat of the pulse, why each man
I have known snapped shut eventually
when faced with the prospect of love,
of a woman right in front of him
who wouldn't take no. And so I must be
content with this model of a man, a training kit,

until I understand what makes *me* tick,
until I can open the door to my heart,
the way I can lift his breastplate up,
and watch myself in motion, the same
veins and arteries, the same blood.

Sweetheart

Lady Devorgilla founded New Abbey in 1273. On the death of her husband, John Balliol, she had his heart embalmed and encased in a coffer which she carried everywhere. When she died, his heart was buried upon her own, which is how the abbey earned the more popular name of Sweetheart.

When I was young I thought the body
would flow on forever like a river.
I can still feel the pain of his passing,
dulled from agony to a sharp tug of memory
now and then. Strange to think,
to me he is still a young man, these forty years dead.
What would he say if he could see me
shrivelled and bent, the girl
who was once his new bride?

We pass through towns with nursery-rhyme names:
Beeswing, Locharthur, Dalbeattie, Kirkcudbright,
where your father met your mother
the summer just after the war.
They greet us with champagne, a sugar cube
fizzing at the bottom of the glass,
to keep it sweet.
Your mother's friends coo
over our wedding photos,
discussing my dress, how handsome you look.
Their fingers are stacked with rings:
engagement, wedding band, silver anniversary, gold.
They will never come off now
over raised knuckles.
They talk about their husbands, how many years
it's been since they passed away.
They tell us how many years they were married,
forty, fifty, all happy. Their children
are grown, gone. They wouldn't stay here,
there's nothing for the young.

When he died, they carried the corpse
to England, but I took his heart, placed it
in a ivory case. I keep it beside me always.
He shares my bed, sits at the head of the table.
For he is still my Lord;
I will always be his wife. I speak
to his heart, ask it to guide me.
I have the best of him; even as the body
turns to dust, I tend his soul.

Lindisfarne

The sky is clear, a real darkness,
every star defined: the castle is reckless
on the cliff edge. They say Madame Suggia
would lock herself in the tiny garret room
and play the cello, its owl call lolling
down the meadow, luring fishermen
to the castle banks, entranced.

I had a picture of this same silhouette,
a full moon, over my bed as a child.
I made a pact with myself
never to set foot on the island
without the man I truly loved.

It would just happen: we would find ourselves
transported to this very spot, ignoring
tide tables, low season. Like the monks,
who came because they heard a voice
that lodged in their bones
and led them here, where the land
welled up beneath their feet.

.

King and Queen

On a transatlantic liner, my parents,
just married, pose for this photograph:
they might be film stars or royalty, the way
my mother offers her profile, gazes somewhere
out of frame, my father leans forward,
stares straight at the camera, business as always.
His hair is beginning to grey. I will be born
a year later. They will stay married, despite
the difference in age, my father's stubborn rule.
In the foreground they are separated by table,
ashtray, handbag. What connects them
cannot be seen, hovers in the air.

I wanted you to promise we'd be happy.
On a hill in Glenkiln, as we climbed
to see Moore's King and Queen, a peregrine
soared above us, good omen for our marriage.
At their summit there was no throne,
no palace, just two figures sharing a bench,
faces complicated, hands not quite touching.
We continued to climb until their distant shapes
became one. From the top, we could see
well beyond their view; it was easy then
to take stock, to map our lives to any route,
the compass unseen, but certain.

The Arnolfini Marriage

The mirror came from a junk shop,
where they called the glass *fisheye*. It reflects
every inch of the room, like those globes in school,
when we peeled off the world like an orange
and Greenland was huge. Since then,
I've had a need to see the whole
picture, the dark corners illuminated.

Like Van Eyck's couple, so secure,
their backs to the mirror, facing the future
hand in hand. We can only believe
they were happy. The artist himself
bears witness-his invention
designed to flatter everything it catches:
more fun house than honest.

*

Mother married me off to a merchant I'd never laid
eyes on until the day, surprised
he'd have me in my state. I wore the green velvet,
high-waisted, to hide my shame.
His Dutch was poor; I have no Italian.

The best artist in town,
hired to paint me in my gown,
took one look at me, grabbed a fold of my dress,
hold this up, like so ... no one will ever guess.

Fish

We followed his path back and forth
through the tank, translucent
blue body, little skeleton
swaying slightly with movement,
bones glowing, an X-ray
of himself, like the fossil

on your mantle, a souvenir of Lyme,
where amateur geologists
tap at cliffs with tiny hammers,
waiting to unlock the fish
left behind in rock,
like footprints in wet concrete.

The net scoops him up.
He is emptied into a bag of water.
The girl hands over a tenner,
carries him off like a take-away.
She disappears into a sea
of broken deck chairs, rusted tools.

I would like to leave
a small trace of myself behind,
so that you can feel the groove
in the sheets, see my face
miraculously redefined in the pillow,
once I am no longer with you.

Birdsong

It was in Woolworth's in Yonkers,
before forty ruffled parakeets rattling their cage
in the pet department, that I first heard you sing.
It was as if you had flown through the door,
their long-lost mother brought back to them
in human form, to ease their restless fluttering,
bring them a moment of peace. And sure enough
within minutes, your singing had coaxed
each and every one of them to sleep.

I wonder if all those parakeets found
owners to love them, liberate them
from Woolworth's, bring them home,
give them names. Maybe they carried your song
on their travels, taught it to their children,
maybe it's known to birds all over New York.
I'd like to think they have the power
to conjure you here, your voice lingering
on the air for an instant, before it disappears.

The Loved Ones

Some say my profession is morbid,
but I see it as a service to the grieving.
My portraits live in their homes, a tribute
to those they've lost. It's not easy
to capture souls from photos, but an artist
must see the things that are invisible.

In my youth, I would draw from life.
Apprenticed to the stables, I admired the grand
tradition of Stubbs, took pleasure in a smooth
flank, a thick mane. I tackled race scenes,
could be spotted with my easel at the hunt.
My reputation grew, I branched out to the hounds.

My first commemorative portrait was an accident;
a Pekinese died during a sitting, I completed
the picture from memory. Her owner, eternally grateful,
paid extra. I advertised my new-found trade:
polaroids of the departed flooded the studio,
with letters that would break the hardest heart.

Some clients still swear that I have captured
a slight tilt of a paw, or a gleaming eye
I couldn't have known. They call it a gift.
Alone at night I often hear the plaintive cries
of neighbourhood strays; I swear my recent Siamese
is calling to them, an anguished, unearthly howl.

And often I have a recurring dream: all my cats
are here with me now, blank eyes old as scarabs,
their new owners dead kings and saints.

St Pancreas

My mother had promised green hills
and sheep, a short train ride away:
we arrived at the gates of a grimy castle, its turrets
spiralling to a witches' watch. Gargoyles hung
from the walls, eyes bulging. I had been excited
about the train, the station with its funny name,
but as we passed beneath the crumbling arch,
I became convinced I would be kidnapped,
hauled underground to a children's prison.
There I would remain in darkness, to be freed
when fully-grown, to wander the streets
in ragged clothes, never to be happy again.
Could Pancreas, the boy-saint, swoop down
like Spiderman to save me, or did he live
inside my body, protecting me from harm?
I knew where my heart was, and my lungs,
I was ticklish in my kidneys, but the strange pancreas
evaded me. Could a part of my body truly
shimmer with goodness, ward off evil and sickness
like an Indian-head penny or a rabbit's tail?
Maybe I had been born without one, how else
could I explain my bad thoughts, my nightmares
I would never be like the boy in grown-up armour,
bearing the standard of the cross—even in the age
of Action Man and GI Joe, his halo never failing
to dazzle, blinding in the face of monsters.

The Jewish Ghetto in Venice

It was the only holiday my mother and I
ever spent together, just us two.
We arrived in the midst of a garbage strike,
other tourists frightened off. Around every corner
that smell greeted us like a guide.

The owner of the pensione took our photo
the day our country bombed Libya.
Your President Reagan is a good man, he told us,
holding up an Italian paper: the only word
I understood was *Guera.*

My father would have panicked, whisked us
off the streets into the Danielli or Gritti Palace,
made reservations in the grand dining room
full of stately old-school Americans, taking grappa
and the *Herald Tribune,* checking baseball scores.

He would never have strayed beyond St. Mark's.
We walked in circles for hours, each turn
a dead end at the island's edge, murky water
lapping the lagoon steadily onshore, clothes lines
tying the houses to each other against the coming tide.

We found the synagogue by accident, no different
to the other tenements leaning into the campo,
took refuge in its musty hall, just as the light
was beginning to fade. The noise our heels made
clattered on the marble floor, echoed off the walls.

What daylight left was blocked by heavy curtains,
except in the gallery where the women
would have gathered. There, the light edged
through high windows, patterning the floor
with latticework like old lace.

We sat there for ages, breathing in the heady scent
of beeswax and brass polish, candelabras gleaming,
dark wood rich, important. We sat where the men
would have sat, a hundred years ago, facing
the ark and its ancient scrolls.

We may have been closest then, in that holy place,
a religion alien to both of us, my father's religion.
It was never mentioned; in retrospect, simply a holiday
without him. Years later, I tried to find the synagogue
again on my own, in that warren of crazy streets,

gave up finally as the light was fading.
It wouldn't have been the same: I could not have felt
the surprise and delight we knew as we passed
into the silent room, as if we had discovered it
and now discovered, we would keep it to ourselves.

The Sighting of the Virgin in Marlboro Township, New Jersey

I have opened my garden to sceptics:
small-time reporters, Sunday drivers, freaks.
The field has become a parking lot,
entrepreneurs have cornered the market
in hot dogs and plastic rosaries.
Their ancestors were the soldiers
who crucified Jesus and the thieves,
threw the believers to the lions,
men like me. They would have sold tickets.

The papers say the Pope himself
is considering a journey to Her shrine,
a concrete statue from Becker's Hardware,
between the toolshed and the pond,
where she speaks to me only on the Sabbath.
Pilgrims have been dazed by light
radiating from Her face, and the woman
who hadn't walked in thirty years
felt a tingling in her legs.

Saint Anthony kept the sanctuary
of his cave, despite the harpies,
the hideous demons, the lusty women
and their siren songs. He must have suffered,
but remained steadfast in his faith.
Until now my life has been uneventful:
She has chosen me as Her clean slate,
a man with no past. I am Her keeper,
I must tend Her garden on earth.

Cactusland

The front from the west has swept into Rutland,
bringing with it the rain which will last all week;
in the heat of the greenhouse, the cacti purr,
each daring us to touch, to test the sharpness
of their tiny spikes, how much pain they can give.
They twist themselves into awkward shapes,
defying the ordinary beauty of flora,
resisting the usual methods of caring.

The gardener's face is lined, like dry earth.
He handles the cacti gently without gloves,
can predict the very moment when small pink flowers
will appear from the depths of their spiky skins.

Outside, the box hedges brave the weather,
crowns of topiary birds and squirrels unfazed.
Gardens display daffs and pansies; friendly,
easy to tend, lining window boxes at the local pub,
baskets at the corner shop. In the churchyard
graves sprout hyacinth, forget-me-not.
You'd never guess the cacti were so close,
dreaming of the day they will conquer England.

The Pub at the End of the World

has no dress code, no Beers of Distinction,
just the local brew, which smells like mildew,
has a head the colour of moth wings.
The walls are a faded yellow, darkened
by nicotine, except around the dart board,
pockmarked by countless failed bullseyes.

There is no jukebox, but a TV
bolted to the ceiling above the bar
is tuned to a documentary on the assassination
of President Kennedy. All three customers
are glued to the car passing the grassy knoll
again and again in slow motion.

You'd have to be lost, cold, badly in need
of a drink, a phone (out of order), but if you
pop in for a pint, the landlord will nod slightly,
watch you from the corner of his eye, wiping
the same glass over and over with an old dishcloth.
You may even feel strangely at home.

There's no last bell. The bar closes
when the final customer gets up to go,
slowly pulls on his coat. A gust of wind
almost pushes him back as he opens the door.
He squints, pauses to make out the pavement,
lifts his collar and braves it.

Chop Suey

On the street people slide through a smudge
of snow and ice, rub their red hands,
watch their words turn breath into steam.
The sky is cloudless, clear: a bad sign.

Two flights up, the women are held in this light.
It inspects every particle of dust, illuminates
their skin, the blush of cold in their cheeks.
Winter is outside; the only reminder, her camel coat,
its fox collar bristling in the radiator's heat.
The restaurant is cheap, reassuring:
the clatter of spoons to bowls, warm slosh of soup,
low voices of other diners rising like a chant.

They have come from opposite ends of the city
to have lunch, together, in the intimacy of chop suey.
One woman leans forward, across the formica,
her back to the room, but something in her body,
the angle of her hat, stresses the urgency of her words,
details only she can know. This is her story.
Her companion listens, ready to provide advice,
sympathy, a related story with a happy ending.

The waiter arrives with a fresh pot of tea,
an orange divided into sections, a fortune cookie each.
By coincidence, their fortunes both read:
everything happens for the best.

Oscar

Caucasian male, early thirties, dead
for at least ten days, the pathologist reckoned,
no sign of a struggle. Through his dirty window,
a view down Skid Row: the grand boulevard,
now abandoned, the old Roxy, boarded up
for years. Its marquee gives shelter
to local winos when a storm brews.

Back then, you could see a feature for a penny.
Tex Avery or Rin Tin Tin or the latest Disney:
Mr. Bill Bojangles singing *Zippity Do Dah,*
a wandering hobo, dancing down
a golden road, holding hands
with little Bobby Driscoll, child wonder,
popular as Shirley Temple once.

He was buried in a common grave,
a potter's field. The Salvation Army
went through his clothes, his few possessions;
there was nothing anyone would want,
except the gold statuette in a shoebox
in the closet. *He could have lived like a prince*
for a week, if he'd pawned it.

Hart Island

I.

Convicts from Riker's who do grave duty
learn to dig deep enough for twenty.
By August, the dry soil begins to crack,
won't give way to a shovel.
But once below the first layer
it gets easy. They work fast;
no markers, no family.

In a few weeks the grass grows again,
dotted with wild daisies, buttercups,
sometimes a bunch of carnations
wrapped in cellophane;
people still make the trip across
on the ferry, don't even know
if they are in the right place.

My grandfather may be there,
or maybe out west; he was last seen
in Kansas, before the Great Crash.
He'd already lost everything.
With him, the letters from his home
also finished—strange, crowded writing
my father couldn't understand.

Now my father sits in his favourite chair,
on the last page of a mystery.
He devours them, reads and rereads,
even when he knows the ending;
old-fashioned whodunnits,
Agatha Christie, Dorothy L. Sayers,
where the story comes full-circle.

II.

The detective lights a cigarette,
pulls his collar to his throat. He's a natural
for this work; never been photographed,
never in one place for long. In his old life
he was nobody, the sort of man
who could slip into darkness quietly,
keep his regrets to himself.

He specialises in missing persons,
traces them by things they've left behind.
Sometimes he rides the ferry to Hart Island,
usually when the real clues run dry;
you can find personal effects piled high
in a dumpster by the pier.
Here is where a case gets closed.

But sometimes a man will disappear
into thin air, leave nothing to prove
he really did exist, except someone's word.
The detective understands this:
you can cover your tracks so thoroughly,
that even those who loved you
begin to doubt you ever lived.

The Box

opens with the faintest trace of your pomade,
a whiff of coconut. At the top I find a publicity shot
against the stars and stripes: war is over, you are
a young Steinbeck, says the *New York Times*.

Novels flow from you effortlessly. There are more
reviews, all glowing. You are invited to launches,
cocktail parties, gatherings of beautiful men,
all poised to write the next great American story.

About halfway down, the box begins to throw out
disappointments: polite rejection letters, manuscripts
never finished, never read, movie negotiations
shelved. The writing grows uncertain of itself:

women wear the wrong clothes, smoke cigarettes
whose brand names have faded to nostalgia.
I find pictures of your lover on the beach,
like a young Kirk Douglas. By now you are forty;

you teach English to Spanish boys who will graduate
to factories. Their cards are carefully written, thank you
for your patience. Your school in Iowa invites you
to speak to students contemplating a career in writing.

Your face becomes familiar to me in old age,
the established family uncle: unmarried, always speaking
in a child's lilt, preferring us to adults. All traces
of your lover disappear; he remains on the beach forever.

The box is almost empty. A nephew will take this drawing,
the resemblance unmistakable. An old friend will claim
the Stork Club ashtray. I will keep the picture

of the stars and stripes. I never knew you like this:
that first flush of success, that double-breasted suit.
The war has ended, the city is experiencing a boom,
and you are about to open a box of shiny hardbacks,
spines perfect, your name emblazoned on the jacket.

Columbus, Georgia

This is the place where Miss Margaret Mitchell
lost her life, your Granny said, as traffic
swerved around her. Safe at home she gave us tea
in dainty cups, then showed us her spare room:
chartreuse, a bed as big as a church,
solid mahogany, she said, *a family heirloom.*

She took us to the house where she was a girl,
where her grandfather hid from Union troops.
We inspected room after room of charred remains:
a baby grand on which Caruso played, cabinets
crammed with blackened plates. Granny claimed
the house was always cursed, even before the fire.

When she died, the Salvation Army collected
her bed; it took six men to get it downstairs,
a hand-carved finial broke in the move.
She was buried in the family plot, her curios
shipped to sons in far cities she'd never seen,
places they discovered to escape from her.

Rossetti's Zoo

After Lizzie was laid to rest
Gabriel abandoned poetry, literally,
to her grave. As she clasped his collected works
to her breast, he roamed the Embankment nightly
like a ghost. The great velvet drapes
at number 16 remained closed all summer,
until one day, he bought a menagerie:
a racoon, a bull, peacocks, a kangaroo and her baby.
He explained to me it was a way of bringing life
back to the old dark house.

Within a week the white bull whose eyes
reminded him of wild Janey Morris
tramped the manicured lawn to bits.
The kangaroo killed its mother, was in turn murdered.
The racoon savaged a neighbour's bantams.
A frightened peahen died under the settee
in the front room. Her mate climbed a tree
and wailed all night. The neighbours outlawed
the keeping of peacocks in Cheyne Walk.
His animals deserted.

For the next eight years he tried in vain
to complete the poems he'd left to Lizzie,
but a preventing force took hold. The buried words
tormented him, the very last he'd ever written.
When he came to me with his plan, agitated,
a man possessed, I though he had gone mad.
I had given my word I would assist
as confidante and friend, so I assured him
I would take command of the ghastly business,
retrieve his manuscript from her icy grasp.

Gabriel was not present when Lizzie was exhumed
in Highgate on that late October night.
I told him later that as the workmen prised
her coffin open, I was stuck by her beauty,
unimpaired even in death. By lantern light
her rich red hair glowed bright, enveloping her
in a shawl of flame. Calmed by the news,
Gabriel returned home and wrote these lines:
The blessed damozel leans out
From the gold bar of Heaven.

And I was never the same.

Stragola

A Transylvanian word meaning 'an unfulfilled soul'.
Local Romanian legend says that stragoli can return to cause trouble
for the living.

At first you couldn't explain the sensation
as my tongue coaxed hairs at the back of your neck,
the chill that crept up the base of your spine
to the nape, as my nails dragged along each vertebra
like a xylophone. But these are merely party tricks.
I will make myself at home inside your every orifice,
change the flow of your blood like a river off-course,
send your feet careening at the precipice,
pound a new beat on your frightened heart.
I will roll out my new-found arts one by one—
such skills can only be mastered if you leave the earth
broken by regret, if you spiral into the underworld
headfirst. You know I did. Now I am dead, you will
relive every minute we were together, every word
you never said. You will feel it now, like the weight
of a coffin lid over your lovely face. I will plant you
here beside my grave, like a weed stuck fast by its roots,
you will lace yourself to my bones for good.

The Cannibal's Lament

I met a sailor one night in Marseilles,
we drank until the small hours and
when he said *your place or . . .*
I didn't hesitate. He tasted salty,
like the sea, there was a capery
bitterness to his thighs, and his liver
was pickled in my favourite ale.

I wanted to talk about the only man
I ever loved. He was an ecologist,
a botanist, a confirmed vegetarian,
cared deeply for animals, worried
about the ozone. He sailed away
to the Pacific Islands to study palms,
I never did tell him. How could I?

My mother was a cordon bleu chef
who grew bored with leathery ostrich,
tough armadillo. My father was always
a violent man. It was self-defence.
She served him with peppers, a touch
of oregano, a fine red she'd been saving
for a special day. It was her greatest.

They shipped my lover back, and I
committed his body to the ground;
he could be one with his precious insects.
I couldn't bear to have him any other way.
I confess, I did steal his heart, made
a beautiful casserole, all his favourite
vegetables. I savoured every mouthful.

The Two Fridas

Frida tore open her chest and heart to reveal the biological truth of her feelings
Diego Rivera

I used to wear my heart on my sleeve
so he could see it beating, panting
like a dog when he walked into a room.
I would turn myself inside out,
display my lungs, my spleen, my brain,
to show him how I'm made,
how little bits of body ticked like clockwork
to push me through the day.

But he was bored, so I churned out
a second girl, to keep him happy.
She looks just like his mother, all laced-up
and haughty. I've split my heart
between us, Siamese sisters, linked
by hands, a strand of artery.
Now he can play with either, play each
off the other, or leave us both.

My half-heart is weak inside her,
quiet like a ghost. She will try to take me
with her, but I am not afraid: our heart
might thread together, I might grow
whole again. I would carry our sorrow
to her grave, and lilies, like the bouquets
he always offers when he crawls
home again, begs me to let him stay.

Barrowland

I have all the time in the world
to play our story once again,
like the songs we knew by heart:
the way you whispered to me
on the dancefloor, light touch
of your breath in my hair,
arms stiff, holding us slightly
apart. You were formal, polite

not like the boy the week before
who'd tried to lead me outside, pleading
cool air, just to slip a hand beneath
my cotton blouse, hook a thumb
under my bra. I'd pushed him away
and left. How I wish I'd let him
take me home, climb beside me
in my narrow bed. It could have been

my secret. But you cancelled out
the others that night. I felt safe
in the back seat of the taxi, all warm
and happy, first time in days;
I imagined my mother asleep in her chair,
a single light blazing through the nets.
Next day she'd still be there, sharing
my photo with the inspector

over a cup of tea. They found me
soon enough, my favourite dress
torn wide, blood caked at the lace trim.
I might have wondered why you quoted
Jeremiah like the minister at church,
why you said the Barrowland was sinful
when you went there every week—
eccentric, I figured, a bit shy.

Now I assemble each bit of your face
to match the Identikit, the freckles
dotting your hairline, light hair
close cropped, lips thin, drawn tight,
I feel them brush one last time on my cheek,
squarish chin, clear blue eyes;
I could see a flash of anger harden them
the moment before I died.

It's easy now to say I must have known.
My plot has a view over the city,
a marker stone, an angel pointing to heaven.
In the distance Castlemilk gives way
to the hills beyond. I'd be my mother's age,
keeper of her brown-edged albums,
clippings she'd saved when I was still news,
when I was always beside you.

The Giant's Lover

(Charles Byrne, 1761-1783)

The signs all over town proclaimed: *the tallest man*
who has ever walked the earth, a full eight foot two
in stockings. He was named O'Brien, after Brian Boru,
ancient King of Ireland. My husband paid two shillings
so we could gaze at him. I did not want to give money to gawk;
I expected a monster, a freak of nature, an act of God's rage.

It is true, I had never seen such a man, or even dreamed
he could exist, had never stared so plainly at a body,
not even my husband's, but I could not control my wonder.
I secretly measured his leg against my own, stood close
so that the brim of my hat grazed his waist. I felt a blush
rise to my cheek; O'Brien never saw me. His eyes held no light.

A few months later, he was dead; his last wish, to be encased
in lead and thrown to sea. He would save his body
from being sold, dissected; his heart, discarded. I dreamt
I could slip out of my stays into fish skin, slither to his sea bed
like a mermaid. But even before he settled to rest,
the resurrectionists were coaxing divers to raise him from his grave.

I will never set foot in Dr. Hunter's museum, even though
my husband says it is the talk of London: I could never face
the sight of O'Brien. I know one day I will rest in peace
inside my tomb, while he is doomed to their gaze. Some nights
I think of him, standing in his glass case, his miraculous body
stripped to its core, his heavy bones no different from my own.

Donor

The prognosis is bad for you:
a heart clogged with the detritus
of living, grizzled and mottled,
purple and blue, so useless
it makes me love you more.

Have mine. I reach through
my sternum and into the cavity,
separate it from the aorta
and pulmonary artery. It is clean,
ripe, ready to do your bidding.

It throbs in my outstretched hand,
a bird that has fallen from its nest.
Without hesitation, you accept.
It slips in neatly, warms to your body,
defibrillated by a single shock.

Easy. Your pulse quickens
with the thought of my sacrifice,
but my love for you has been drained
with my blood: I am
listless, cold to your touch.

Jumbo

I'd never dreamed of running away to the circus,
like other girls. Even at six I thought clowns
had no dignity; I could see the grey
beneath their day-glo wigs. Now I know them,
know they've worked up and down the country,
as short-order cooks, lumberjacks,
after their wives took off with the kids.

The circus is where you land when you're through
in the real world—it happened to me.
At the trailer park I met Estelle, who toured
forty years with the Tarantella Brothers.
She still spent an hour every morning drawing her lips
in Pango Pink, tracing the line of her brows in Flame,
to match her hair. She could see I needed the work.

I started out as the candy girl, each night picking
caramel popcorn off my skin. Did a stint on the trampoline,
until my fall. Finally I worked the elephants,
got a spangly costume, a long striped stick
to guide Trixie and Jumbo into the ring.
I liked the deliberate way they moved,
their sombre, old faces. Life was good,

until the day we arrived in Woodlake. They greeted us
with handpainted signs about animal rights,
didn't care about Frederico with his lions, or Marie
who rode her palominos bareback, loved them like kids.
That night they waited for the last light to go out in camp,
then began to free the animals one by one;
Marco the lion was so afraid he hid in the woods,

staggered back to camp at dawn. The police finally
found them all, except Jumbo. The call came at noon;
he had been spotted lumbering towards the edge of town,
dried blood down one leg. The sheriff drove me past
clean white clapboards sporting stars and stripes,
lawns that looked painted, to the other side of the tracks,
its familiar shacks, rusted pick-ups cluttering the yards.

He'd fallen exhausted right in the road, its white line
interrupted by his huge bulk. A crowd of gawkers
had already parked themselves along the grassy bank.
I almost wanted to sell them peanuts.
A keeper from the local zoo was trying to cool him down
with a long hose. He lay very still, legs folded beneath him,
his breathing heavy, irregular, shaking the hot asphalt.

I don't know if he made it.
I slipped away from the sheriff, escaped to the woods,
which stretched as far as the Interstate. I raised my hand,
made the sign I'd used to signal Jumbo back to his cage.
The first guy who stopped was towing a U-Haul
behind his Chevrolet. I didn't even ask him
where he was going.

Ticonderoga

A box of one dozen extra hard Marvelead
Dixon Ticonderogas, with Ethan Allen,
Hero of 1775, poised for battle on the front:
when opened, they stood to attention, precise
yellow and green stripes capped with erasers.
The sharpener was bolted to the edge
of the desk, ready to receive its recruits.
As I cranked the handle, the pencil became
itself, I could smell the rich lead, the shavings
of its labour, making a point just for me.
A fresh sheet of paper, straight blue lines
guiding my careful letters slowly over the page.

Each morning we would stand beside our desks,
place our hands over our hearts and recite
the Pledge of Allegiance. I could repeat the words,
but didn't understand *republic* or *indivisible*.
Our teacher wore green trousers, a polyester top
with yellow flowers, and a pendant that said
another mother for peace. It was the year
the National Guard were called to Kent State,
a war raged in a country far away. Chalk dust
coated the linoleum, our drawings of mommys
and daddys, houses with chimneys puffing clouds
into a bright blue sky, a sun always smiling.

Biology

The first incision was the worst, the way
my scalpel sank into the strange grey flesh,
the stench, the pig's eyes shut tight,
as if he couldn't face the indignity,
his vital organs exposed. Mr. Ormanati bent over
my pig, so close I could smell mints on his breath,
trace the mound of his humpback through
his brown polyester jacket. I longed to touch it,
to see inside his refrigerator, where he kept
his insects; *cold, they are easier to dissect.*
Sometimes he left the closet door ajar
and if I craned my neck I could just see
his foetal deer, asleep in its huge glass jar.

Each night I'd drag the textbook to my room,
stare at diagrams of musculature until my mother
said goodnight, then by flashlight I'd find
my dog-eared Havelock Ellis, real life stories
of every kind of fetish: shoe sniffing, grown men
in diapers, animals, paedophiles, necrophilia.
By day I'd study the postman or the butcher
hoping they'd betray some hidden desire,
or the boy in my class who sometimes stared back
when Mr. Ormanati touched the curve of the female
reproductive system with his pointer, pronounced
fallopian softly, like the name of a song.

Arrowhead

Judy's dad must have been past sixty by then
but he still ploughed the field each season.
We'd follow his dust, sniffing the fresh earth,
mining what the ground gave up: shiny mica,
sharks' teeth, arrowheads filed to a fine point.
I had a drawer filled with bird skulls, fossils
from the time the land was underwater—
I imagined my house at the bottom of the sea.

We learned the Lene Lenapes were a minor tribe,
the first pacifists. The boys were disappointed,
they'd wanted scalps. It figured even our Indians
would be boring. They wanted facts and battles,
a sense of history riding through them.
Instead we intoned the names of presidents:
Washington, Jefferson, Adams; a litany of
capitals: *Albany, Salt Lake City, Des Moines.*

I tell my stories to invest them with gravity,
now I understand the way each year dovetails
into the next, how memory sharpens a single day:
*the field is reeling where I stand, the damp smell
of earth, the arrowhead big in my little hand.*
I want it now, to squeeze tight until the tip stabs
the skin. I want to send it flying, so it may show me
what I've missed, piercing the heart of everything.

vanilla called out to me
a comforting monotony
it wore as thin as ...
...
... were

Plain Jane
my mother's middle name
is in the family

running £5 on binge

you called me
you called me sweet
you called me ...
you vanilla
you called me ——

we fought our battles over
ice-cream, calling me
vanilla; calling me cold
stomach churning on an
emptiness. the

I carry in me the surname of my
my mother's middle name
a maiden voyage; ... an onto-chime
the ___ to be called plain Jane
the anchoring

the maiden
voyage of a
dinghy
ship paired
navy
'plain
Jane'

Vanilla

was always my favourite flavour
until mini skirts and minted breath

vanilla

was always my favourite flavour
until sorbet came along

About the Author

Tamar Yoseloff was born in the U.S. in 1965 and has lived in London since 1987. Her pamphlet collection, **Fun House**, was published in 1994 by Slow Dancer Press. She has won the London Writers' Competition twice, and third prize in the Peterloo Poets' Competition. Her poems have appeared in various anthologies including **The Forward Book of Poetry 1994, As Girls Could Boast** (1995), and **Jugular Defences** (1996), as well as in a number of magazines. She was the book review editor for *Poetry London Newsletter* from 1995 - 1997 and founder of the *Terrible Beauty* poetry series at the Troubadour Coffee House in London. **Sweetheart** is her first full collection.

Other Slow Dancer Poetry Publications

Lucille Clifton
The Terrible Stories
ISBN 1 871033 42 X 72pp £6.99 (UK only)

Lee Harwood
Morning Light
ISBN 1 871033 41 1 72pp £6.99/$13.95

Dream Quilt: 30 Assorted Stories
ISBN 0 9507479 4 7 48pp £3.00/$6.00

Rhona McAdam
Old Habits
ISBN 1 871033 21 7 64pp £5.00 (UK only)

Martin Stannard
The Gracing of Days
ISBN 1 871033 09 8 56pp £3.50/$7.00

Ruth Valentine
The Tide Table
ISBN 1 871033 46 2 64pp £6.99/$13.95

Slow Dancer books should be available in all good bookshops.

Representation UK:
Signature Book Representation
2 Little Peter St,
Manchester M15 4PS
Distributed by Littlehampton Book Services

Representation USA:
Dufour Editions inc
PO Box 7
Chester Springs
Pennsylvania
19425-0007

Or order directly from
Slow Dancer Press
59 Parliament Hill
London NW3 2TB
tel/fax (00 44) (0) 171 435 5964 e-mail slowdancer@mellotone.co.uk
Please add 50p/$1.00 per item P&P